Contents

Introduction

The Indian subcontinent is home to an incredible 700+ reptile species. The desert sands of the Thar, beaches and oceans of the Andamans and dense rainforests of the Western Ghats are rippling with reptile life. They come in every size and shape, from thumb-sized geckos to car-sized crocodiles. Every single one of these species is perfectly adapted to life in our diverse subcontinent.

What makes reptiles different from other animals?

Reptiles were the first animals with backbones to not just make the leap from ocean to land, but also fully adapt to terrestrial life. They've been around for a long time as they emerged over 300 million years ago! Reptiles have scaly, waterproof skin and shelled eggs that can survive out of water. These key cool characteristics let them leave their aquatic ancestors behind.

Reptiles play vital roles in maintaining nature's balance and ensuring that our ecosystems thrive. Reptiles can be both predator and prey, keeping all sides of the food chain in check. Herbivorous reptiles help disperse seeds and fruits, allowing plants to flourish. They're very useful for humans too! Snakes are some of nature's most important pest control measures. Helping keep rodent populations down. Lizards hunt down insect pests too.

Are reptiles in trouble?

Unlike birds and mammals, reptiles are mostly cold-blooded. Their body temperatures match those of their surroundings, though some reptiles can change this a little. They need to use tricks like adapting to different habitats, basking in the sun or even hibernating to keep their body temperatures in the right range. But climate change is affecting seasons, making summers hotter and winters shorter. Because reptiles rely on external temperature more than mammals, this could impact them a lot.

The cold-blooded metabolism of reptiles is the ultimate efficiency hack. Maintaining a warm body temperature takes an awful lot of energy. Warm-blooded animals consume way more food than cold-blooded ones. This lets reptiles survive where others would starve. Waterproof scales, hardy eggs and unique jaws are other special features. But being dependent on the heat of the sun for your body to wake up can also be a handicap that reptiles need to learn to live with.

Western Ghats King Cobra

CRITTER STATS

Scientific name: *Ophiophagus kaalinga*

Size: usually 3–4 m long – as long as a small car

Weight: 4–10 kg

Habitat: forests, fields and even urban areas

Lifespan: 17 years in captivity

Conservation status: vulnerable

Between dense grasses, moss-covered tree trunks or on the forest floor, you may catch a glimpse of the king cobra. Black and white, brownish grey or even an olive green, it blends in with the shadows. Step carefully – you might see it rear up and spread its hood!

The king cobra reigns as the undisputed ruler of the serpent kingdom, a cold-blooded assassin that feasts exclusively on its own kind. When snakes are scarce, it might feed on lizards or birds.

Occasionally, you might see the king cobra flick out its forked tongue. It's not to taste the air, but it's a way for the snake to smell better!

This snake also relies on its sharp eyesight. It watches and waits, spotting movement from a distance. Once it spots prey, it pounces like a tightly coiled spring released.

The king cobra bites deep with long, sharp fangs. These fangs contain venom which quickly affects the prey's nervous system. Soon, the prey can no longer move.

If the cobra catches a large animal, it might go months without eating again!

DID YOU KNOW?

Although a king cobra's bite can be deadly, they try to avoid people as much as they can. King cobras bite only when threatened, like when accidentally stepped upon.

For a long time, scientists thought that king cobras were all one species. Newer studies have led them to believe that there may be four different species of king cobra! The Western Ghats king cobra is one.

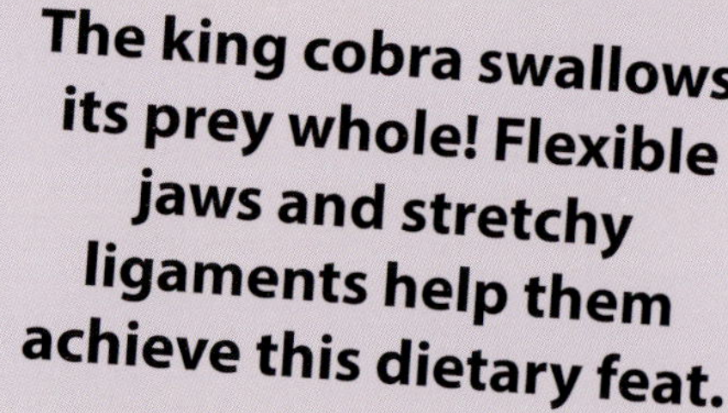

The king cobra swallows its prey whole! Flexible jaws and stretchy ligaments help them achieve this dietary feat.

Mugger/Marsh Crocodile

CRITTER STATS

Scientific name: *Crocodylus palustris*

Size: 2–3.5 m long – as tall as a double door fridge if made to stand on two legs

Weight: 30–120 kg; average weight is 70 kg

Habitat: marshes, lakes, rivers and artificial ponds

Lifespan: 20–30 years

Conservation status: vulnerable

From irrigation canals in agricultural fields, to salty seaside lagoons and freshwater wildlife sanctuaries, the mugger crocodile can survive almost anywhere. With thick, muddy brown scales and a long, terrifying tail, the mugger looks like a creature from the Jurassic Park movie!

Despite their bone-chilling reputation, mugger crocodiles are solar-powered sunbathers at heart. To power their cold-blooded bodies, these reptilian giants sprawl across riverbanks, soaking up sunrays.

They are smart hunters. During bird nesting season, muggers balance sticks on their snout.

Unsuspecting birds swoop in to investigate. Might this stick be good for a nest? Then, CHOMP! The "stick" becomes a trap in one lightning-fast bite.

Muggers are good parents. Most reptiles walk away once eggs are laid. In contrast, mugger males have been known to help stuck hatchlings out of their shells.

Mugger parents work together to help their hatchlings into the water under the cover of the night. They take care of their young for almost a year after they're born!

It's not genes that determine the sex of baby muggers, but temperature! Cooler nest temperatures produce females, and warmer temperatures produce males.

The skin of the mugger might look tough, but it's very sensitive! It helps crocodiles sense vibrations in the water, helping them "see" when things get murky.

Muggers rate riverine restaurants a 5/5 every time. From fish to unsuspecting cattle, birds, turtles or even other crocodile eggs, this reptile will eat pretty much anything.

Pope's Pit Viper

CRITTER STATS

Scientific name: *Trimeresurus popeiorum*

Size: up to 80 cm – as long as a desk

Weight: unknown

Habitat: forests in mountainous regions; common in patches around streams and ponds

Lifespan: unknown

Conservation status: least concern

The Pope's pit viper is one of the most striking sights in the forests of the Eastern Himalayas, a living jewel coiled among the leaves of treetops. It moves silently through canopies and undergrowth, relying on patience, camouflage and precision to catch its prey.

In the bamboo thickets and dense forests it prefers, it's hard to catch a glimpse of the elusive Pope's pit viper. But with its wide red eyes and "pits", you can be sure it's caught you!

Like the leaves and stems around it, the pit viper's body is a bright, vibrant green.

Pit vipers have a specialised heat-sensing organ known as a "pit". It lies between the eyes and nostrils. These pits function like built-in thermal cameras, detecting the body heat of nearby animals.

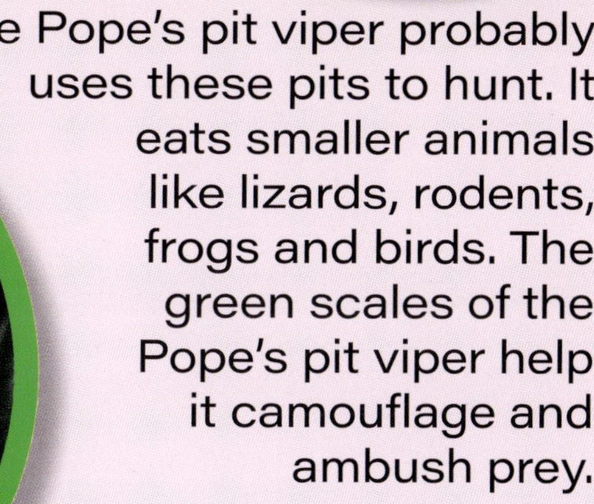

The Pope's pit viper probably uses these pits to hunt. It eats smaller animals like lizards, rodents, frogs and birds. The green scales of the Pope's pit viper help it camouflage and ambush prey.

The Pope's pit viper has venom! It's a hemotoxic venom, which means it affects the blood stream of bitten animals. Scientists are working on an effective antivenom.

This snake isn't named after a Vatican Pope! It's actually named in honour of two American herpetologists, Sarah H. Pope and Clifford H. Pope.

Unlike most snakes, the Pope's pit viper is viviparous! This means it gives birth to live young.

Olive Ridley Turtle

CRITTER STATS

Scientific name: *Lepidochelys olivacea*

Size: the turtle's shell is 45–65 cm long, as big as a cabin suitcase

Weight: 35–45 kg

Habitat: open ocean; they nest on beaches

Lifespan: 50–60 years

Conservation status: least concern

An arribada or mass nesting of olive ridleys in progress.

Small, green and heart-shaped, the olive ridley sea turtles spend most of their lives in the open ocean. Under moonlit skies, thousands of turtles come ashore together in great numbers to lay their eggs – a yearly cycle of life and return.

The story begins under a blanket of stars. The mother buries the eggs in the sand. Tiny hatchlings break free to emerge into a world bathed in silver moonlight.

They navigate using the reflection of the moon and stars dancing on dark waves towards the sea.

Thousands are born; only few survive. Seagulls and kites swoop in to catch a snack. The hatchlings must beat the birds to the ocean. And then escape the many hungry fish.

Once they're adults, an incredible process happens. It's like turtles have a perfect map in their heads.

Using Earth's magnetic field, they return to nest on the same beaches that they were born on.

Olive ridleys don't always return as lonely pilgrims.

Sometimes, hundreds arrive together in a spectacular reunion called the arribada. Quiet shores transform into bustling maternity wards as the turtles lay their own set of eggs.

Olive ridleys' favourite foods are jellyfish, snails, crabs and shrimps. Occasionally, they'll go for an ocean salad and dine on algae or seaweed.

Although sea turtles need to surface to breathe, they can spend a long stretch of time underwater. Olive ridleys can dive to depths of 500 feet and more.

The olive ridley is one of the smallest sea turtles, but the most abundant by far! They're found all over the world. But that could be threatened in the future by loss of habitat and climate change.

Indian Chameleon

CRITTER STATS

Scientific name: *Chamaeleo zeylanicus*

Size: about 20 cm – like a pencil; the tail can be another 20 cm long

Weight: up to 100 gm

Habitat: fields, dry forests and scrublands

Lifespan: 3–7 years

Conservation status: vulnerable

The Indian chameleon moves with a slow grace in the quiet branches of trees. A close observer will see minute moments – eyes that swivel in different directions as it watches the world, skin that shifts colour and a tongue that strikes like lightning!

The chameleon's reputation as nature's master of disguise is a myth. These living rainbows don't shift colours to vanish into their surroundings.

Chameleons wear their hearts on their scaly sleeves and broadcast their emotions in brilliant technicolour. Scientists have recently discovered that most of the chameleon's colour changing is for communication.

The colour change might even help them regulate their body temperature. Darker colours can absorb sunlight and warmth.

Even though they don't camouflage and ambush prey, the Indian chameleon is a formidable hunter. They catch a wide variety of insects like crickets, grasshoppers and termites.

Indian chameleons are also famous for their slow dance. If you spot one at rest, look carefully – it'll probably be swaying slowly from side to side like a boat adrift.

DID YOU KNOW?

Female chameleons descend from trees to lay eggs. They carefully dig tunnels to lay eggs, before returning to treetops.

Each of the chameleon's eyes follows a different story! Their eyes move entirely independently, working separately to capture as much information as possible.

The Indian chameleon has an incredibly long, sticky tongue. This can be even longer than the chameleon's body! It shoots out to nab food.

Bibron's Coral Snake

CRITTER STATS

Scientific name: *Calliophis bibroni*

Size: 50–65 cm – as long as a guitar

Weight: unknown

Habitat: wet forests in high mountains

Lifespan: unknown, but most other coral snakes live around a decade

Conservation status: least concern

The Bibron's coral snake is a small but striking resident of the high, misty forests of the Western Ghats. Secretive and venomous, it spends most of its time hidden even in the dead of the night. When it emerges, you're rewarded with a shockingly beautiful glimpse of bright red, with stripes of black.

For the slender Bibron's coral snake, life is a constant game of hide-and-seek where losing means becoming someone else's dinner. Larger snakes and raptors are its greatest enemies.

But if it wanted to hide, why is this species so colourful? The snake's back is almost a blindingly bright red, with dark black stripes.

For some animals, bright colours can be a form of protection. They say "stay away" in the most vivid way possible. They warn predators that "I'm venomous, toxic, dangerous or maybe even all three!"

This small predator packs genuine venom, using it to hunt other snakes. The venom doesn't seem to be too dangerous to humans.

Though small and secretive, Bibron's coral snake plays a big role in its ecosystem. Its bold colours and quiet presence remind us that danger can come beautifully wrapped in the wild.

Unlike some other snakes, coral snakes can't retract their fangs. Their fangs are also brittle, and may break easily. This might be why the snake is so shy and elusive! Fights could end up being costly, and it could end up losing its key weapon!

Coral snake venom is neurotoxic. This means it affects the nervous system of prey, paralysing them and making them easier to snap up.

Indian Star Tortoise

CRITTER STATS

Scientific name: *Geochelone elegans*

Size: 15–35 cm, the length of an adult's shoe

Weight: usually 1–2 kg – but can be up to 6 kg

Habitat: dry areas, scrub, fields and grasslands

Lifespan: 35–80 years

Conservation status: vulnerable

The Indian star tortoise is a small, gentle and shy creature. It's active at dusk and dawn, but can make a daytime appearance during the monsoon. The star tortoise is instantly recognisable, thanks to the constellation-like pattern on its shell. The dark brown shell is covered with little stars, with yellow lines connecting them.

If you're in a grassland, dry forest or scrub at dawn or dusk, keep your eyes peeled. A gentle rustle, or a slow shift might be a sign that the Indian star tortoise is around.

It is crepuscular, and is most active as the light fades from the sky or at dawn. Its characteristic black and yellow pattern offers the perfect camouflage, helping it blend in with the shifting light of sunrise and sunset.

Armed with a delicate beak-like mouth, this gentle herbivore grazes like a miniature lawnmower, methodically harvesting grasses and fruits. But when times get tough, it even samples dung.

Unfortunately, the once-common star tortoise has paid the price for its beautiful appearance. One of the world's most heavily trafficked animal species, they are caught, then shipped out of India and bred in various countries as pets. They are also losing out as their scrub and open habitat disappears.

DID YOU KNOW?

The Indian star tortoise has the rare ability to right itself if it flips over. The unique shape of the shell and a strong push from its legs is all the star tortoise needs to get back on its feet.

Female star tortoises are much larger and heavier than the males. This extra weight probably gives them the strength to lay clutches of almost a dozen eggs!

Males compete for mates by trying to flip each other onto their backs. This might be one reason they're so good at flipping back – lots of practice!

Indian Spiny-tailed Lizard

Find Me Here!

The Indian spiny-tailed lizard lives exclusively in the northern deserts of India, mainly in Rajasthan and Gujarat.

CRITTER STATS

Scientific name: *Saara hardwickii*

Length: 30–40 centimeters, about the size of a large laptop

Weight: 180–200 gm

Habitat: hot, dry desert

Lifespan: likely 10–15 years

Conservation status: near threatened

To spot the Indian spiny-tailed lizard, you have to be quick on your feet and sharp with your eyes. This sandy brown lizard blends perfectly into the deserts and grasslands it favours. The only telltale sign of its presence are burrows. Spot one, and you have a good chance of seeing its owner!

This reptile is like a bodybuilder. Instead of strong legs or shoulders, this lizard flaunts a tail so chunky it looks like it's been lifting weights with it.

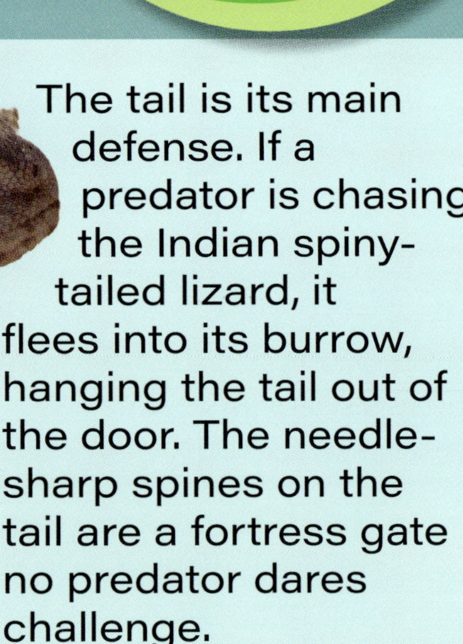

The tail is its main defense. If a predator is chasing the Indian spiny-tailed lizard, it flees into its burrow, hanging the tail out of the door. The needle-sharp spines on the tail are a fortress gate no predator dares challenge.

This tail is a lifeline — in times of scarcity, the fat stored in the lizard's tail comes to its rescue. The lizard can survive for a while using this fat store.

Each lizard lives a solitary life. They're territorial, and chase each other from their burrows.

Unfortunately, the lizard is also hunted for its tail. People make oil from this fat which is believed to have medicinal uses. As a result, this animal's population has declined a lot.

DID YOU KNOW?

Burrows are climate-controlled, protecting the lizards from the hot desert sun. It's like an apartment with a great AC – no wonder they act like tough security guards!

The Indian spiny-tailed lizard is India's only herbivorous lizard! It feeds on the flowers and fruits of the khair plant.

The high fat content of the lizard's tail makes it a prized snack for desert predators – like a candy bar for kites and eagles.

Dog-faced Watersnake

CRITTER STATS

Scientific name: *Cerberus rynchops*

Length: around 60 cm – as long as one stride

Weight: under 1 kg

Habitat: mangroves, mudflats and tidal pools

Lifespan: unknown

Conservation status: least concern

"Dog-faced Water Snake" is an unusual name for a snake. How can a snake be dog-faced? And what is a water snake? But one look at its snout and the ease with which this reptile swims through mangroves will give you all the answers. Though mildly venomous, it's shy and rarely bites – more swimmer than striker.

Life in mangroves rises and falls with the tide. As the tide comes in, roots sink beneath the waves and life scurries back into the treetops. As the tide falls, movement resumes and the dog-faced water snake emerges.

This aquatic assassin is an incredible ambush hunter. It often hides in burrows and crevices. Fish, eels, crabs – anything moving nearby is fair game.

Multiple snakes sometimes gather around one tide pool. As the tide rushes out, many fish get stuck in the pool, cut off from the sea. They are then easy pickings for the waiting snakes.

Mangrove habitats are challenging to navigate – its hard to get a grip.

The dog-faced water snake has finely keeled/textured scales that help it grab onto and grip mud. They also sidewind, a special sideways movement to move across mud.

The dog-like appearance of this snake is actually an adaptation for its life under water. As its eyes and nostrils are placed higher up than in other snakes, it can breathe and swim during high tide.

You might have heard of crocodile tears, but the dog-faced water snake is a reptile that cries much more. They drink freshwater as much as possible, but occasionally drink salty water. Excess salt is secreted through glands on its face.

Dog-faced water snakes pull fish from tide pools out onto the land. These die on the land, becoming easy prey for the snakes to snap up.

Maritime/ Mourning Gecko

CRITTER STATS

Scientific name: *Lepidodactylus lugubris*

Length: 8.5–10 cm – as long as a stapler

Weight: likely less than 50 gm

Habitat: tropical rainforests and coastal forests

Lifespan: other *Lepidodactlylus* species live for 2–5 years

Conservation status: least concern

All images in this chapter are taken outside India.

With a slender body and velvety smooth brown skin, this dainty gecko looks like an elegant statue. From its snout to its eye lies a dusky stripe, almost like eyeshadow applied by a master makeup artist. The maritime gecko is tough to spot, but well worth the effort.

In the dark of the night, the maritime gecko darts from treetop to treetop. Its skin, which is in shades of soft browns, even changes colour with the gecko's mood, helping it blend in with the shadows.

The maritime gecko is a survivor to its core. It isn't picky, dining on everything from insects to spiders, fruits to flowers, or even an unsuspecting human's snack cupboard!

What's even more incredible is this gecko's ability to clone itself. Every one of these geckos is female. So no courtship dances, no searching for mates.

Adult females clone themselves, laying one to two eggs each time. The eggs are perfect copies of their mother. Very rarely, a male might accidentally be born.

Scientists think this trait might have helped the maritime gecko survive in situations where mates were rare. This could be due to the small gecko numbers on the tiny islands that this lizard loves.

The maritime gecko is native to South and Southeast Asia, but has become invasive in places like Hawaii! Its ability to clone itself has ensured that this gecko can survive anywhere.

Unfortunately, the maritime gecko's dainty appearance and hardy nature has made it prized as an exotic pet.

Female maritime geckoes lay 1–2 eggs at a time. The eggs stick tightly onto trees, crevices and corners. They're said to be particularly fond of Pandanus palms.

Follow the pug marks to find some of the best places to spot India's amazing wildlife!

Fact Finder

Ahmed, A. (2017, June 15). *The Coral of the Western Ghats—JLR Explore*. https://jlrexplore.com/explore/naturalist-s-corner/the-coral-of-the-western-ghats

Dedukh, D. et al (2022). Premeiotic endoreplication is essential for obligate parthenogenesis in geckos. *Development, 149*(7), dev200345. https://doi.org/10.1242/dev.200345

Denny, K. L. et al (2023). Communication via Biotremors in the Veiled Chameleon (Chamaeleo calyptratus): Part I – Biotremor Production and Response to Substrate-Borne Vibrations. *Integrative and Comparative Biology, 63*(2), 484–497. https://doi.org/10.1093/icb/icad085

Dinets, V. et al (2015). Crocodilians use tools for hunting. *Ethology Ecology & Evolution, 27*(1), 74–78.https://doi.org/10.1080/03949370.2013.858276

Fisheries, N. (2025, May 29). *Olive Ridley Turtle | NOAA Fisheries* (Pacific Islands, Southeast, West Coast). NOAA. https://www.fisheries.noaa.gov/species/olive-ridley-turtle

Gamble, T. et al (2015). Into the light: Diurnality has evolved multiple times in geckos. *Biological Journal of the Linnean Society, 115*(4), 896–910. https://doi.org/10.1111/bij.12536

Geochelone elegans (Star Tortoise). (n.d.). Retrieved 20 July 2025, from https://animaldiversity.org/accounts/Geochelone_elegans/

Gerry Martin. (n.d.-a). *Dog-faced Water Snake: Sludge and Salt in the Intertidal Zone | Roundglass | Sustain*. Retrieved 20 July 2025, from https://roundglasssustain.com/species/dog-faced-water-snake

Gerry Martin. (n.d.-b). *Indian Chameleon and the Art of Disappearing | Roundglass | Sustain*. Retrieved 19 July 2025, from https://roundglasssustain.com/species/indian-chameleon

Gerry Martin. (n.d.-c). *Mugger: River Monster or Peaceful Giant? | Roundglass | Sustain*. Retrieved 19 July 2025, from https://roundglasssustain.com/species/mugger

IUCN. (2011). *Calliophis bibroni: Srinivasulu, C., Deepak, V., Shankar, G., & Srinivasulu, B.: The IUCN Red List of Threatened Species 2013: e.T177549A7454847* [Dataset]. IUCN. https://doi.org/10.2305/iucn.uk.2011-1.rlts.t177549a7454847.en

Janaki Lenin. (n.d.). *Croc Creche: Why Crocodilian Males Make Great Babysitters | Roundglass | Sustain*. Retrieved 19 July 2025, from https://roundglasssustain.com/columns/crocodilian-males

Marshall, B. M. et al (2018). Hits Close to Home: Repeated Persecution of King Cobras (Ophiophagus hannah) in Northeastern Thailand. *Tropical Conservation Science, 11*, 1940082918818401. https://doi.org/10.1177/1940082918818401

Mourning Gecko (*Lepidodactylus lugubris*). (n.d.). iNaturalist. Retrieved 21 July 2025, from https://www.inaturalist.org/taxa/104226-Lepidodactylus-lugubris

Nania, D. et al (2020). Continuous expansion of the geographic range linked to realized niche expansion in the invasive Mourning gecko Lepidodactylus lugubris (Duméril & Bibron, 1836). *PLOS ONE, 15*(7), e0235060. https://doi.org/10.1371/journal.pone.0235060

NIF Team. (n.d.). *India's Striking Variety Of Pit Vipers | Nature inFocus*. Retrieved 19 July 2025, from https://www.natureinfocus.in/animals/india-s-striking-variety-of-pit-vipers

Nisarg Prakash. (n.d.-a). *All about Spiny-tailed lizard | Roundglass | Sustain*. Retrieved 20 July 2025, from https://roundglasssustain.com/species/all-about-spiny-tailed-lizard

Nisarg Prakash. (n.d.-b). *Dog-faced water snake: Facts, Diet, Habitat | Roundglass | Sustain*. Retrieved 20 July 2025, from https://roundglasssustain.com/infographics/dog-faced-water-snake-facts

Nisarg Prakash. (n.d.-c). *Indian Star Tortoise: Facts, Diet, Threats | Roundglass | Sustain*. Roundglass Sustain. Retrieved 20 July 2025, from https://roundglasssustain.com/infographics/indian-star-tortoise-facts

Nisarg Prakash & Diviya Mehra. (n.d.). Indian Chameleon: Facts, Behaviour, Diet | *Roundglass | Sustain*. Retrieved 19 July 2025, from https://roundglasssustain.com/infographics/indian-chameleon-facts

Philippines, M. T. (2024, October 21). Four of a kind: King cobra is a quad of species, not one, study finds. *Mongabay Environmental News*. https://news.mongabay.com/short-article/2024/10/four-of-a-kind-king-cobra-is-a-quad-of-species-not-one-study-finds/

Tandon, A. (2024, November 7). The lizard caught between myth and modernisation. *Mongabay-India*. https://india.mongabay.com/2024/11/the-lizard-caught-between-myth-and-modernisation/

Deepak, V. et al (n.d.). *Redescription of Bibron's coral snake, Calliophis bibroni Jan 1858 with notes and new records from south of the Palghat and Shencottah Gaps of the Western Ghats, India*. Retrieved 20 July 2025, from https://www.researchgate.net/publication/255180841_Redescription_of_Bibron's_coral_snake_Calliophis_bibroni_Jan_1858_with_notes_and_new_records_from_south_of_the_Palghat_and_Shencottah_Gaps_of_the_Western_Ghats_India

Vyas, R. et al (2025). Notes on natural history and conservation of the Indian Spiny-tailed Lizard (*Saara hardwickii*). *Reptiles & Amphibians, 32*(1), e22562. https://doi.org/10.17161/randa.v32i1.22562

Credits

Writer: Yamini Srikanth

Designer: Abhishikta Dutta

Picture Credits

iStockphoto: 1181603645, 1290211815, 1187750278, 2227530501, 1256132476, 1172928833, 1172928836, 1172929398, 1174424491, 1329069694, 1164898538, 1175019259, 1091652684, 1239138222, 494445888, 1192387938, 1479676790, 1479676423, 1164856252, 1164856581.

Wikimedia Commons: King Cobra by Abdulla Al Muhairi and Kalyanvarma; Mugger Crocodile by Dr. Raju Kasambe; Pope's Tree Viper by Rejoice Gassah; Indian Chameleon by M. Arunprasad, Shantanu Kuveskar, dineshkumar7, Mike Prince, vijaybarve and Anjan Kumar Kundu; Bibron's Coral Snake by Prasenjeet Yadav and Sandeep Das; Star Tortoise by Thivanka Ilanperuma, M Kooragamage and Davidvraju; Indian Spiny-Tailed Lizard by Muhammad Musab Malik, Raja Bandi and Raja Bandi; Dog-faced water snake by Md. Tareq Aziz Touhid and Md Sajjad Hossain photography; Maritime Gecko by Brown R, Siler C, Oliveros C, Welton L, Rock A, Swab J, Van Weerd M, van Beijnen J, Rodriguez D, Jose E, Diesmos A, Tim, luluchouette, Mário NET and Christian Ferrer.

iNaturalist: King Cobra by kalyanvarma and ramitsingal; Pope's Tree Viper by rejoicegassah; Olive Ridley Sea Turtle by tejayantrapalli, phoekman and danharville, Indian Chameleon by dineshkumar7; Bibron's Coral Snake by ramitsingal; Indian Star Tortoise by sai_shailesh; Indian Spiny-Tailed Lizard by ashwinv, pkishore and rohitmg; Dog-faced Water Snake by tejayantrapalli and prathamesh2; Maritime Gecko by carey_knox_southern_scales and aggie_wildlifer.

Pexels: Two crocodiles and a bird standing on the grass by Hussain Niyaz.

Independent Sources: King Cobra (top image, pg. 7) by Dhritiman Mukherjee; King Cobra (image on pg. 6; top image, pg. 9) by Romulus Whitaker; Mugger Crocodile (top image, pg. 11) by Mrunal Deolalkar; Mugger Crocodile (bottom image, pg. 11) by Madras Crocodile Bank Trust; Baby Mugger Crocodile (bottom image, pg. 12) by Utkarsha Manish; Baby Mugger Crocodile (top image, pg. 13) by Prakash Kannan; Mugger Crocodile (middle image, pg. 13) by Anjana Srimathi; Olive Ridley Turtle (image on pg. 18) by Bipro Behera; Olive Ridley Turtle (bottom image, pg. 20) by KS Seshadri.

Map: Syailendra Gupta Muliawan, India Vectors by Vecteezy.

First published by Juggernaut Books 2026

Text copyright © Indian Pitta Kids 2026

10 9 8 7 6 5 4 3 2 1

P-ISBN: 9789353459284

E-ISBN: 9789353459703